vast.

by Benny Woith

I've rewritten this twenty times. I can't seem to think of what to write. To ease you into this. My mind. There aren't really many words that would help. Maybe, **raw.** Like severed meat, it's clawed deep into my wounds, maybe yours.

Wherever the road leads you, know that I'm here. I've been broken. Mended. Raked like leaves. I know you have been too or else you wouldn't be here.

This book is the vast space of the breathing I've done on this earth and I don't want to apologize for it. And I won't.

- Yours, Theirs, Mine

FIRST

My words.
Their words.
They get lost.
The lost silence.
I could paint the silence.
Use it to fill up these holes.
Puddle it out of cracks.
Use it to shine the silver.
To mend the broken glasses
that were on your bedside table
next to that book you've been reading.
The one with the pages dog-eared.
The pages that spoke to you when I could not.
For my life is full of silence. Of being it.
I want to speak out.
Have someone listen.
Then maybe they could dog-ear me.
Or put me into their pocket.
Pick me like a dandelion and blow.
Make wishes off my parts,
my individual dreams.

I'm thankful for words.

IN THE TRENCHES

We don't have a chance.
To be strong for our babies,
our loved ones.
Our houses aren't being set on fire,
our mouths starved for days.
We forget the aching ancestors.
Their guts ripped clean,
the heart beaten raw.
The heroes
we no longer live up to.

We've become lazy
without even trying.
It's become easy.
Our feet
slipped deep
under warm,
safe covers.
Our voices and freedoms,
now mobile
and permanent to our sides.
We are our own worst enemies.
We are our own war.

So get a move on,
grenades are lining every shore.
But I beg you,
please,
ask for more, more, more.

THE FEMALE

The Female is the mother of lucid beauty, a connoisseur of the lonely. It is the bust, the jaw, a calf, a shoulder, a caress, a walk of exquisite shadow and light. It is worth a bloody good fight. It is the sadness. It is the loss. It bears the burdens of yesterday, today and tomorrow. It experiences the sorrow, draws pain out of the marrow of the bone, the bones you call home.

The Female is delighted love. It rather you do the talking, the knocking on Its door, laying down the floor so It can have a place to dance. It knows you like It to dance. Swaying with laughter as It delicately twirls and twists to an unknown singer. You want It to linger.

The Female is breath. Pockets of warm clouds, that pillow circles around your soul. Calming fears you never knew, healing wounds that once were blue. Blue is a shade that never looked good on you.

The Female is a silent savior. It resides in the depths of your beating drum, the one you call the hum that pumps red like Its dress. It is rest, the solace of a secure rope, a line that caught the right one this time. And time is never enough, and Its lips you won't tire to touch. It is the rush. The flame, the tide, the wave goodbye, yet It will return. For the Female can't help but yearn. You give It the spark it needs to burn.

The Male is a mystery. There is comfort in Its strength and quietness in Its open spaces. It's distracted by splendor, possessed by the curvature of beauty's soft neckline. Proposes everything but matrimony, digs just far enough to bury you waist down. It's muck all around, yet 360 degrees of arms to melt arguments, reduce blows.

The Male is perhaps a rough symphony. Cymbals, trumpets announcing an entrance, a presence. A back talk, eye rolled, sighing concerto that hits the highest note of retreation. But you come back for the elation, like a Beethoven, a cloud number ten. Just when you think It's finished, just when you think it's time for bed.

The Male is a coffee ring on a table. Once desired, tasted and sipped, now leaving with nothing but a smudge, this grudge, the time it took to nudge you out of the dream and realize the male is frustrating scenery.

The Male's history is unwavering, Its wink so savory. Its time is not on time. Its voice brushes coarsely yet will soothe at whispering octaves. Lush dimpled, golden fleck eye, the cause of our cry, how Juliet could think to die.

The Male is pursuit. A goal, a touchdown, this home run, to run home to. You do. Just do. The Male looks good on you.

UNDER

I kiss like a fish.
With your mouth the bait.
Oh, how your fingers drown me.
I never want to wake.

CALL LEDGE

My university is of life.
Seeing every violent heart
beating crimson bursts
spread wildly
among the busy streets.
Catching like vibrant fires,
inflaming words,
creating verbs on the city's pages.

The rainbow waved graffiti
of the artist's mind
splattered and swept
across the dirty walls.
A visual antidepressant.

These lessons learned
from the heavy breath
by the gentle mother of mothers,
their memories thawed out
and served like warm apple pie
straight from the cerebral oven.
Their anecdotes and late-night jokes
raised thick with accents
lost now beneath the texting type.

The pop quizzes
pursued by the grit of a working man,
his daily sweat and grime
sticks proudly to his jean overalls,
the hay residue still there from the stalls.
There's true poetry in their speech,
the tired lines of hard lived lives.
The kind unsolved in a classroom,
never found in libraries.

HOOK HER

Luxury is in the know.
It is charming
but silenced by dress.
Intelligence nestled
in every thin mistress.
Hidden impressively
by laced lips.
They pretend to be combed
by innocence.
But find themselves
in empires of stone.
Placed in cheeky tears
and tonight's lust.
Shattered by this intruder
called touch.

A DYING OCCUPATION

I'm too independent,
no man needed.

Woman.
Broken and unclean.
Furnished till the death
with all the things,
the men swear they need.

My woman comes out in a stillness.
I am not the eager, brazen, broad I appear to be.
No.
Delicate my flowers petal.
Uttering beauty and substance,
begging for a renaissance.
A re-do. A re-play.

Sometimes I wish
I could keep the girl inside me at bay.
She runs around all day,
laughing and exploring her life away.

If only I could be moderate, composed, clean.
You wouldn't have to come find me.
I'd be still.
I'd be feet sunk deep in this spot.
You could catch me.
But then would I be happy?

POSTCARD

Welcome to my life.
Step right in.
Mud on your shoes?
Stomp on my carpet.
Bleed on there to.

(I want to remember your name.)

GOOD FOR GONE

You have all the fun.
You close the doors slamming in you.
Answer the call you received that was overdue.
But I need you,
to feel something too.

You have all the fun.
I want it though it's wrong.
Please don't break me in until I'm done.
And we run, we collide, smother our insides.
Painted in each other's blood.
Crimsoned in the flood.

You have all the fun.
You have me until I'm done.
Expired, severed dry and battered thick.
Heaved sick and left just as quick.

I'm caught, netted fish and flesh.
I'm such a mess, hair dripping wet.
And we've just begun.

You have all the fun.
You should slam the door and run.

ART

Paste it together
with macaroni and mud.
Paint it with
your sweat and blood.
Say that it's a work of art.
And overprice
your "bleeding" heart.

HURRY

I am the source of bewilder and baffle.
I stroke the cheek of console and conceive.
The mother of gluttony and grievance.
I am a whore of a hurricane.
I spread open houses,
destroy the contents of the consumer.
Whimper acid tears,
then try and maneuver.

THIS IS WHAT I COME HERE FOR

Everything is so close to me.
On the surface of my skin, the terrain of my being.
Everything I'm seeing is making these lines and becoming
intertwined in my soul.
And I ask for more.
This is what I come here for.

Give me more.
The lack of your luster.
The competitive filibusterer of our vision.
The prism that cuts the rainbow of our birth.
The girth of its colors, all over the pages, our covers.
This is what I come here for.

To rust out the iron of your mouth.
The blood of its bath
and the aftermath of its tongue.
Let it run, run until its faucet's undone.
And we've only just begun.
Perhaps I've found the one.
This is what I came here for.

I've done it sly and slow.
Going unnoticed
palms and parties
I no longer attend.
I've been on the mend.
Pressuring my kettle to hiss,
managing to forget a kiss or two.
Do... do.

I figured out you would not do.
Do.
The things I asked of you.
Because I ask plenty and volume.
I don't think to call you
anymore.
Because I'm on
the move.
It's moved me on
but I can't help but be caught
lavishly and long
between your voice and song.

I'M NOT COUNTING

Today, it doesn't stop.
I'm going to let them run
like the rivers bursting forth in body.

I have fallen in love with guitars,
the fingers that pluck their chords.
The hands that shape their boards.
The eyes that come forth
and cut the seams of averages.
The legs that saved the lives.

Yet, I have been blinded
in touch and turmoil.
The cheated conversations
that ended in "No".
That began in "Don't go".

They have seen me at both ends.
Lungs exhaled in breath
and inhaled in the relationship's death.
There have been enemies made
at the front lines of the beauty.
Of wealth and duty.

I have bitten the lips of men
who try to forget they gave in.
The waves caved in
and the both of us lost the tide.
That point where we break down and hide.

You have taken my picture,
I've deleted your number.
Gotten new covers,
while you, other lovers.
The nights and its brothers
that keep me awake.
And grab the very space
that now is cold. I'm old.
When all these years went by.
So many men's hearts that had to die.

I have decided to leave myself to the right side.
The side that is designated
for the mastery of love.
This love that eludes.

I conclude it is the greatest mystery known.
That a man is worth more
than the heart you loan.
And the lessons learned
gives marrow to the bone.
The one that's broken,
the one that will mend.
That will bend
under pressure and pleasure.
They mend, we mend, I mend.

Let us begin.
Start all over again.

BATTLEFRONT

Don't expect men to call you.
Or fall over you.
Don't expect them to
eat, drink and sleep your presence.
They have their own agenda.
Do expect them to dangle you like jewels.
Ride you around like mules
and pretend like it's the man's way.

Don't react to their kind words.
Lies will keep you up at night.
Never trust a man who breaks promises.
Might as well be hearts.
Not your heart, love.
Not your heart.

Tell yourself, you're detached.
The ribs are your shelter.
Your barricade to go on another day.
Use words like cannons.
Position your eyes away from the bang,
the *BOOM*.

Never let them touch you.
Never let them close
because once they come in
there's no going back.
No going back, love.
No going back.

Ready,
aim,
attack.

CARNIVAL

Broken ears
barking at the door.
Fingers finding your bridges,
crossing them.
Fraying at touching lips.
Smoothing hair with kisses.
Crashing knees together
like tambourines.
Colliding bones
like bumper cars.

DIAL TONE

I ache for anything that's next to me,
I ache for what's beneath.

Even your long frowns and jagged teeth.
The ones that dig now into another's meat.

Because we are the everything I ache for.
The lines drawn, pitch perfect,
because I have yet to believe
you're not worth it.
My back is just that to you,
a place to stab a knife into.

When I ache for what's next to me,
the you and me.
Know that I ached
for what was beneath.

There is a slow withdraw
of self in relationships.
You hope that each time is different.
That each smile you give
is unique and memorable.

But it becomes stagnant.
Like the other.
One from each other.
You regret every kiss
you gave and received.
Every time you leave.
Door shut smooth.

For the now and then
is always expiring.
You're finding more reasons
to play catch up.
Hatch up a new plan to get away.
Even if they want to stay.
And they do.
But can you?

Can you?

ROOM

There's distance between people
that we create.
Each of us with subtle baggage
and weight.
I work so hard at perfection,
I fail before I even start.
But isn't it enough that my heart is in it?
No. No.
I don't think so.
We fan the flame of emptiness.
I fan the flame of emptiness.
Just barely enough room in there for me.

I imagine it a large room.
With the window, open.
Fresh air to blow the chime.
The one that helps me wake.
And though I may not show you or tell you,
know that my heart was in it.

I don't make pretty very much.
The bud of my soul wishes
for someone to understand its root.
That the stretch of me is too vast and long.
That the inside of my body
will express itself all wrong.
These tangles and taboos collide into you,
at faster paces than you're used to.

The emptiness of my room
can only hold the solar of me in it.
And the distance created between
you and me is merely because
I can't get through the door
I've built to fit it.

I feel the heartbreak in your beats.
The echoes in its waves.
I see the emptiness your body produces by
the closeness that you crave.
And I crumble from exposure,
I waver from its seas.
The vast space of your sadness
seems impossible to please.
I hear the chatter of your talking.
The lazy of your stride.

If they told you,
you were undeserving of love.
Please know,
please believe,
please understand,
they lied.

OWNERSHIP

Does your body belong to you?
Does it do what you tell it to?
If the man comes over and through,
Does your body belong to you?

INSOMNIAC

You don't block the window anymore.
The breeze is cooler
without the thick sweat of your breath.
Air more fresh,
not stained by the dirty words delivered.

This space kisses me in ways you never could.

BONE BRUSH

He cripples the brittle cream dust
that was my bone and blows it,
yes, blows it until gone.
Until all that was left of me was air.
There I flew, free but no, you don't see me.
Yet I'm in you now, breathed in and not found.
Hidden in turns you never uncovered,
between your deepest regret and greatest lover.
I still see her there, standing, lengthy and taunt.
Strumming the side of a glass on top your heart
while sinking her lit cigarette
into your right atrium.
I just hide and it's soft and dark,
except for her flame.
Which I feel will never die out.
But I'm foreign and confusing.
I'm deep and reality.
Your reflexes beckon me upward
to the thick layers of your throat.
The soft pink tissue of you clings to my pieces,
like army wives to their camouflaged husbands.
You release me *(sneeze!)*
forcing me from your body,
the dim light from her cigarette
casting a glow from your larynx.
Like a light to guide me home.
Or maybe to send me out alone.
I am so small. Transparent. I'm not even there.

Where?
See, here.
No.
I'm nowhere.

TAME ME

The oldest story I've heard is that men
would be lining up the block for me.
No, they are expired.
They are spoiled milk and moldy bread.
Men don't line up.
They gather in thick and uneven numbers for safety.

Because I am a raging river they can't contain,
a fever they hope won't remain.
The secret sliver of light between the day.

The oil of their dreams,
Laced with streaming pools of dark.
Black holes of tepid fear and exhaustion.
It's clear they aren't packed
for this kind of expedition.

Lining the block for me?
No.
They are walking past me,
head down, sweating terror.
Cornering blocks of trepidation and turmoil.
Unable to accommodate my fire.
Worried they don't have enough fuel for my flame.

I'm miles away now,
throwing sparks across the kindling,
bursting light among the land and sea.

Tame me? No dear, no.
They can't even name me.

CENTS

I'm so tired that even
love
makes sense.

Thinking of kisses
I've never had.

Men
I've never met.

You have never seen this side of me.
That wanders.
Gets lost in strangers.
Intimate whispers.

MORAL GROUNDS

She's dripping
from head to toe with beauty.
You lick her bones dry.
Her sweet curves make you lie
to me.

You produce them
like woman produce babies.
Loud and thick.
Sweaty and smoldered.

I'm wringing my heart out.
It's not a doormat anymore.
Because for you
I can't be a better whore.

And don't I wish I was your pretty?
Don't I wish I was your flesh?
Don't I wish I could cause you an uproar
like all the rest?

SEVEN

Jealousy is a humorous beast.
It taps its claws down the corridor of your body.
Ticking reminders of what it can destroy.
Consuming any decency you hope to enjoy.
Rocks intensely back and forth
the infant of turmoil.

It is designed to decay the inner lining
of your wealth in merely its soil.
Raging wars against humble and harmful.
It is an armful of rotting flowers,
with thorns still intact.
It is envy with fangs.
And it remains.

Until you get a bigger door.
Adorned with confusing locks and thick chains.
Something made of steel.
Something real,
like gratitude and acceptance.
Represent it at as a deep concrete wall.
Make it something the beast
will never be able to crawl.

I find that addiction in all its forms
tends to parade itself around like hard work,
but it is bitterness and resentments.
It likes to gorge itself on bowls
of heartache and lust.
With the spoon of gluttony.
It cuts down clean on the skin of pain
and bleeds out the tears of words
and questions we fear make us human.

Yes, we are human
but we bare ourselves naked
only for showers,
only to rub raw clean
the stench of reality.

Please bare yourself fresh.
The flesh open to beatings that heal.
I promise they will heal.

Take speed and aim
for the bull's eye of a rebirth.
Desert the addictions
and let them dry.
Let them thirst for tears
you will no longer cry.

BABY STEPS

I've forgotten what it's like to crave a kiss.
To wait impatiently for the warmth to come.

First, listening to the thick rolling fog
of his voice brimming from his lips.
Watching them form candied words
and liquored nothings.
Which could become poetry with a pen and paper.

And I sit and wait for his last word to form
and I know it is his last because I can't wait anymore.

I had forgotten what it was like to kiss.
Baby steps, touching flesh.
Getting the hang of this.
Again.

And I beg to not regret it
and I will fight to keep it alive.
This time.
I promise this won't be a waste.

No wait.
Again.
I'm not done with your taste.

MOVE ME

Life gets uninspiring, generic.
Like a cereal box
you really don't want to open.
You kind of just leave it there,
the cartoon on front expiring.

You think only in movies,
do people buy plane tickets spur of the moment. Only
prostitutes named Vivian
get the high-class prince.
That blonde girls from California
can pass Harvard.

These tales, their woes, their money loans
make you feel life is too common.
We can't rob banks and get away.
We can barely get away
with our stuff after a breakup.
And you never want to get out
of a dream you've made up.

But when I look up there's no stars to wish on,
no sunny skies.
After I rub my eyes,
I see only office ceiling and buzzing lights.

INTIMATE KILLER

I remember
rubber bands around the wrist,
learning how to kiss.
Wondering how other people made love.
If their bodies ever got stuck together.

If you might get stuck to me and if so,
would you like it?

But people are haunted.
Like buildings.
Like prayers.

And even if I learn how to speak like you,
my accent still getting thicker,
you would no longer understand me,
or fit me in the cracks of your teeth, your molars.

And if this is how people make love,
with speech,
with preaching.
I should snap for remembrance.
Learn from the pain.
The red lines.
How they swell with pride.

I remember now.
Even while making love,
people always hide.

Sometimes when I walk alone in the city at night,
I think about how I would get raped.

Would I struggle?
Fake a convulsion?
Try and repel them
by drooling all over myself?
Laugh in fits of wild hysteria?
Bite the neck and draw blood?
Would I silently enjoy it?

I pass by a younger couple,
their little boy's laughter.
And I feel safer.
Somehow.

I guess I learned then,
there's safety in numbers.

I GRIEVE FOR THE ECHO

I don't expect much now.
I've deserted the thought
of wishes and hope.
I hold fast and let go
because it seems easier to cope
with the intense need of someone.

I can't be first, this won't work.
I have better things to do.
Like become painted with loneliness.
Watch it mark my walls and floors.
The handles of doors.
Can't let myself give in.
No, watch me get out.

Sleight of hand, *(caressing you)*
no, get out.
Watch me leave.
I have a heart to retrieve.

I can't be first.
I can't be first.
I won't be first.
But I have this thirst.
And you've got oceans for eyes.

ROLE PLAY

My mother says
I shouldn't play
with the big boys.

But I'm caught between
my youth
and her voice.

I'm being parted
both ways
like lips.

Taught to
flatten my breasts
and put away my hips.

I am no longer mine.
I am now yours.

But mother said
you only want
better looking whores.

GOALS

I want to get knocked up
by punching bags.

Get wasted
with garbage cans.

The phone to ring simultaneously,
because they can never get enough of me.

I am a perverted poet.
Who honks for lovers.

Blows cigarette smoke in
shapes of heavy artillery.

Grenades are like sweet candy.
They give me beautiful cavities
for my canines.

AK-Forty Sevens
whip through my halves like loaves
of lukewarm lieutenants.

I'm all the legal you can handle, baby.
For a million light years.
And the current stars
haven't even reached us yet.

WALL, THEN STREET

The man walking toward me,
he won't move.
He's assured I'll do the side swiped,
lily white, head down, dance around.

He's got a full plate today,
he knows I will understand.
In fact, he doesn't even think of me,
and maybe not even see me.
And that's ok.
Because I see him.

Thick necked, tie tight, circulation fight.
Haircut costs more than his clean shoes.
Suit debt and phone full
of all the numbers he'll never call.
Too afraid to really pursue one and fall
in love with something.
Bleed outwardly and all.
On knees bent he'll bawl,
night's suffocation closing in,
as he drinks down
multiple dollar sign liquor to fit in.

I feel rivers for him.
Rushing forward and out.
I understand severely what he is all about.
I turn around and watch the fight he'll lose.
But I see him, and tenderly, fiercely,
I embrace his wounds.

DEAF IGNITION

Do my curves remind you of their valleys?
The way I pronounce a word.
Does it prick the inside
of your ears like hot needles,
retelling of their lips?
The taste.
Your sips of their cool water.
While mine may only be lukewarm.
And if I pour myself over you,
do you suffocate?
Do you carry the furnace of your heart,
heavy and burning
to every room you both shared?
Bared shoulders and stares.

This doesn't, does it?
You don't, do you?
Am I really new?
Am I new to you?

UNRAVEL

The circle of life propels itself outward.
And the journey back again is longer
and harder
but you walk it.

You're flattered and then flattened.
And in that order
or else it would be easy to say no.

No, because you've been here.
No, because you didn't like it.

It didn't suit you. Didn't tie you in.
There are so many knots,
you don't know where to begin.

So, you sit in the middle of your room,
and unravel.

Someday a fellow traveler will help you
but until then,
just sit and unravel.
For everything that you couldn't win.

ARM ME

I bought a gun today.

Sleek, smooth silver weight
between my wrong and right.
I never spoke a word of love to you,
my island, desolate, an empty sight.

As quick as you put one foot into my sand,
You decided fiercely that it had no worth.
So, I put the barrel to my heart
and shot cleanly where it hurts.

No more is it a part of me.
I can finally breathe
and I do not bleed.

It is just sand that starts to pour.
As the smoke from the weight soars.

BAGGAGE CLAIM

You pick me up and drop me off.
Like a sneeze, a habitual cough.
I test your waters
but you've got lessons to learn.
And women to burn
through.
And you like to disable yourself.
Withdraw from the deep oceans.
If I cause a motion,
you get sick.
Pick which struggle to carry quick.
Which baggage to claim,
which debt to pay.
And I can't compete.
I don't like to lose.
But you need more time
and you can't choose.

VACANT

I'm not allowed to call you home anymore.
I'm not to linger your sidewalk
or admire your gardens.
You no longer pick those flowers for me.
I can't ring the doorbell
or knock on the solid wood door.
My key no longer fits in the lock.
I'm trying to convince myself
I don't want it to.
That I don't need your sturdy frame,
open windows, your warm fireplace.
They now belong to the next renter.

Don't tell her
I put too many holes in the walls.
Or that I muddied the floor.
Just tell her,
I don't call you home anymore.

SELF

He will take care of me.
Will take care of me.
Take care of me.
Care of me.
Of me.
Me.
I will take care of him.
I will take care of.
I will take care.
I will take.
I will.
I.

GROWING DOWN

Age is everything and a number.
It dictates and abbreviates
a possible fairytale ending.
Pretending it's doing you a favor.
Saving you from a paper signed final.
Sheltering you from denial
that in the end it's all for the best.
You can rest peacefully next to a mutual party.
Mutual Bacardi breath,
left doubting everything's existence.
Like your resistance to falling in love again
is a choice brought on by lack of faith.
That someone,
anyone is going to bring you there safe.
Age is everything and the number.
And isn't that a bummer?

WEATHER OR NOT

I never pay attention to the weather.
Only to things that affect me
and the weather never does.
I can handle a rainstorm in a dress
and a heat wave in black slacks.
There are more important things to worry about.

Like calming the anxiety of the human heart
or holding the hand of the friend who's lost a child.
Those are different kind of weathers.
Greater storms that require attention.

There's decency that gets lost
in the urgent need for umbrellas
and token rain boots.
Or a perfect day for shorts and shades.

This obsession with weather
tends to make us greedy
for everything to be better.
And if we can't admire
the ironic snowfall on a summer's day
or the crack of sun
through the clouds on a hail storm,
how are we meant to deal
with the greatest storms of all?

I'M NOT A GOOD PERSON
BUT I HAVE HOPES FOR THE FUTURE

This is the pit, the hole, the trench
that I've shoveled hard and fiercely went.
Because it was safe and secure,
so I thought
and their arms felt whole
but their lies cut sharp.

Years and years of scars
drove me to even darker bars,
the clingier men,
the violence there in
and I waited for the liquor to settle
and then win.

And it did
and in there
I hid.

REM

I can't just dream
of normal things.
The doorway opens,
yet it's who it brings.
There's not rest here,
for only the wild sing.
This plague of turmoil,
among the fresh leaves.

I can't just dream
of a lover's tender kiss.
Their lips like sandpaper.
Voice of a snake's hiss.
Full army of heartache.
As they all fire and miss.
The joker at the party.
Full of wine and piss.

I can't just dream
of a happy ending.
The audience inaudible,
while the actors pretending.
You still have me caged.
Locked away, demanding.
Sleep is but an endless hole.
All the while I'm descending.

I THOUGHT OF YOU

He dropped me off and I thought of you.
I thought of all the things we couldn't do.
I stopped it before it began.
And you ran, ran, ran.

He kissed my lips and I tasted you.
Lips round the rim,
closed and thin,
time didn't stop with him
though.

I thought of you,
over and over of you.
All the things he made me do.
I grabbed my thighs and thought of you.
I hushed my sighs and thought of you.
I cried my eyes, thought of you.

And all the things you didn't do.

SUFFICIENT

What do you need me to be for you?
Tight lipped, both ways.
Baby making babooshka.
Lace, push up bra.
Blonde hair like straw from over bleaching.
Teaching myself to stay over,
roll over, and then play dead.
Begging for you, when I need to be fed.
Coy, self-mocking, dandelion
blowing wishes for kisses that don't come.
Like myself,
I don't come often enough to be won over.

You have yet to play the game.
But you are in fact playing games.
Just not ones that I have the rules for
or want to participate in.
Because you want to salivate at the distance.
You missed it.
You weren't watching,
but you don't have my channel anyway,
or feel the need to find it.

What can I be for you,
when you don't even know?
You've dealt a hand that I can't match,
not because it's too low
but because it's the wrong suit.
Yeah, we're cute.
But so are bunnies
and honey, I need more than surface layers.
I've had too many players.
I don't need enough for a team.
I'm just looking for something
that wakes me from the dream.

What can I be for me?
Everything.

SCALE A TON

I turn down the street.
It's just a noise or the certain smell
and I'm back to something else.
To him, to him, to him.

These streets hold as many memories
as cigarette butts, as pieces of chewing gum,
greyed from all the cars running over them.

With reality looming as a knocking door.
Each time, I think it's better than the time before.
And it's not. It never is.
His fiery kiss will always be missed.
But so will his and his and his.

There's no more space in my body
for all these lovers.
I can't give away anymore.
I've got no meat left for me to eat.
They are ravenous and I let them come.

I'm too tired to not let them have their way with me.
Relationship? Sure, give me three.
I need to feel wanted and won.
So I let them finish me, until I'm done.

BOOTY CALL

You might as well
just leave your panties around your ankles.

In fact, take them off altogether.
They already have you ready.
They think it's easy access from here on out.
Men are capricious.
They create the walls,
design the house,
and then don't let you out.

Unless they got what they wanted.
Then there's nothing left to write back for.

Yeah,
just forget the clothing at home.

In fact,
make it the phone.

She's the right shade of night-time.
She's the angle of the glass in the moonlight.
She gets all the you, you let by.
She gets all the you, you give.

How lucky the floors that feel her feet,
or the brushes that run themselves
through her hair and teeth.
Or the bra that cups her breasts so neat.
She gets all the you, you give.

Her chest a place you could lay your head.
The safety net caught between the wall and bed.
Yet you choose the wall and tried to forget.
She gets all the you, you give.

The laughs she collided with your grin.
Couldn't prepare you for the all the emotion
you would feel there in.
You pushed her away before she could even win.
She got all the you, you give.

If you stare at the wall hoping for peace,
the feeling of loss will not decrease.
She gave what you needed, yet still you ceased.
Now only with the you, you gave.

RED ROPE

Every night I remove you from my brain,
Untangle the red rope you gave and then frayed.

Hoping wild horses could trample me clean,
for my heart craves weight, my lungs not to breath.

Each morning, there is so much space to fill.
I cannot continue to hope that someday you will.

And I won't be another lover for you to boast.
So, I catch fire to the rope and then
let
you
go.

I live wide open.
Like a prostitute token.

Bleeding virgin soaked
innocence.
There's no more innocence.
I've never had it.

Rid myself of badness.
My brain, damaged.
My revenge, savage.

And now I have to go on,
like you never touched me.
Like I've survived nothing.
When all I want to do is die.

EXPIRED

My body isn't getting any younger
and I worry about where it will fit in.
Between the sheets, nestled close to you.
If you wish I had the body
of my twenty-three year old self.
When I was pounds thinner and less bitter.

I'm running out of time.
No one can love me for just my insides.
Lusting for livers and gushing for gall bladders.
No, they will only see what they want to see.
The outside me.
The one faced with lack of eternity.
And I bite my tongue till it's bloody,
because I can't force it.

There's not even anyone to rush anymore.
No one is knocking on my door.
I think my neighborhood is lost.
Stuck in another dimension and tossed.
Thrown away like the garbage
I surround myself with.
Like the garbage I relate to.
I'm just old gum and rotten food.
My expiration date is long past due.

You are bigger than me.
Both of torment and reality.
You have brought me back to me.
Like the distance of my parts
came home to each other.
As if they could never imagine another.

You are bigger than me.
I'll convince myself, you're not poison.
Because my eyes are bigger than my reason.
And maybe it's just for a season.
I want to have you hold me through the cold.

But I am bigger than this.
And I don't want to always wish
myself through the winter.

TATTOO

I've marked you.
On the side.
So I don't come back.
A sign to tell me what is fact.

No, no I'll never come back.
You can communicate
with every medium.
Through time and space,
I'll never read them.

I won't come back
and this time I mean it.
Maybe someday
you'll believe it.

THE NEW THINGS

She looks good.
Right, fitted tight for you.
And I'm happy.
Happy for you.
Finding the one,
like I knew you'd do.

You all do eventually.
And they are never me.
They are certainty,
where I was only monopoly.

The pit stop, to halt.
Waiting for your inspiration
to restart
and I jumped it for a while.
My electricity wild,
unless the spark went out.
Each time, and without a doubt.

You all use me for the shock factor.
Strolling around with walkable fire.
Feeling brave,
arm in arm with a dutiful and static liar.

But then I burn for nothing
and I'm not fun anymore.
I'm dark and dirty.
A smudged ash whore.

DIRTY DITCH

I'm
fucking
everyone
I can.
Just to rebel
against
your scent.

To replace
every
lingering
finger
you laid on me.

The strokes
of bruises
you left on me
now lay buried
under
a million
other men.

RELIEF

It's a relief.
I don't have to believe you're it anymore.
Or that I found you attractive.
Or be reactive to your hopes and dreams.
They used to include me.
But now you told me they don't anymore
and my future is wide open.

But did I mention that it's a relief?
Yes, the biggest relief yet.
I don't have to sweat around you,
worrying about my body lasting too long
or my kisses coming out wrong.

Wondering how I would belong,
in the closet of a space you gave me.
In the life, you built to persuade me.

You're a relief not to come home to.
And now I'm free to come home.

VEIN

I return back to the self,
myself was before you
and it calms me down.

I was a human
before this was fake,
I was a person
before we fucked.

Before you entered my body clear
and removed yourself bloody.
But then, I can recreate new blood,
that is the beauty of the body.

HER DULL

I envy her innocence.
Her unassuming resistance.
For she does not know you like I do.
She will know you like I do.
And she will smile because she's forced to.
Just like I had to do.

I can't sleep and I blame you.
It's too hot to fall in love anyway.
And your body still heats me on occasion.
Maybe someday it'll be months
before I'm still being burned by you.

JUST WAIT

I worry about someone I've never met.
Does she know about the faces you made
when you crawled inside of me?
When your oil inked arms held me down
into the blackest of nights.
Even with sun through the shades in the day.
Hearing the laughing kids outside play.

Did you tell her
I was the hideous monster?
Tall shadows in your night terrors.
The face of your mama, the fists of your papa.

I would describe to her,
the way you sound when the hour is too much.
When your demons
have been coating your soul all day.
Thick and vengeful, hissing.

Is she scared yet?
Does she regret the bed you share?
How the king size mattress, feels like a twin now?
How you won't give her room anymore?
You are the room. You are the floor.
You will shut the door and never let her out.

I wish I could tell her,
"Don't forget his birthday.
Don't go out with your girlfriends.
Don't ask for time alone.
Don't withhold.
Don't remain cold.

Open yourself daily
to the lashes of his tongue,
sharp cuts of wet violence and warm venom.
He will cut you daily.
With or without your hands.

Just let him buy you things.

Let him spoil the space
of your world with suffocation and status.
Until you owe him everything.
Whenever he wants it.

Honey, he owns you now.
Just close the door.
There's nothing out there
for you anymore."

HELP

They don't tell you,
that therapists are hard to find.
They don't tell you,
because they don't even talk about it.

It's never a topic of discussion to ask for help.
To need it in someone, even just to unload.
To lay out each layer of your baggage wound tight
on the table and allow someone to help you dissect.
All you need is someone to help you digest it.

They don't tell you much. People.
They just say fine,
"Yes, we're fine.
Life is fine.
Work is fine.
Kids are fine.
Dinner is fine."
Lying.

Because we're too much right?
We can't be seen
deserving.
Of anything.

I just need someone to talk to.
Someone I'm paying to listen.
Someone I'm giving my money to.
Who knew that this would be so hard?

Abuse was easy. Suicidal thoughts were fine.

But this, this is the greatest struggle of all.

THE KNOT

If I ever get married,
I will have learned vulnerability.
The heavy lump of bitter and disaster
I kept rumpled in the corner of my room,
will be folded and put away by another.
Without shame or apologies.
Just silky words.
Touching cheeks with purrs.

If I ever get married,
it will be about time.
How I love you's aren't first date material.
They are letters earned
and syllables graduated in honor.
Made by the toughest of armor.
Worn by the respectable and sought after.

If I ever get married,
I will have had enough guts
to say no and even better,
a yes to the yes that felt right.
Not just for the night.
But for a lifetime and the middle sponge.
The one that soaks up all the love,
that cleans where you hadn't thought of.

That lasts not just the wedding.
Not the first kiss.
Not just a spark,
the fire or flight.

If I ever get married,
it's the meat of my heart.
The flesh from my bones.
The right,
Right.

WILD CHILD

How much of the internet is making us all into the same person?

We have the same choker necklaces, felt hats and brown shoes. We buy from the same stores, own the same phones, text the same emojis. We take photos of meals at the right angles, ask others to hold the camera to our faces.

Hoping to be recognized.

We went here, we saw this. We enjoyed it. We swear we did. Here let me show you.

We're not lost. We have maps for that.

How much of your day is spent tracking other's days? How much of the minutes that make up your life are from scrolling your time into oblivion?

When did we stop being these vivid, untouched creatures of wonder and exploration? Driven by reclusion and wild thoughts.

Why now, are we on the conveyor belts of the media, the CEO's, the debt collectors. The ones who steal our time, our energy. The buds of flowers we haven't ourselves planted. Because we're so use to being given bouquets of plastic and polyester. Someone telling us, it's just as good, if not better.

Who determines us? Who dictates what we share with the world? When our own imagination is chipped away by Facebook and Twitter. Our beliefs buried underneath the backlash from this false wall we call freedom of speech.

You're barking to a box baby, you're screaming at a screen.

Listen. Bum bum bum. Do you hear that? That's you. In there. That's the dream. That's the shovel sunk deep within that loose dirt. The noise it makes. The soft crunch of depth and deliverance. You are unhooked. Removed clean from the wires which connect you to the drug of being seen.

See yourself. Listen to yourself. Fight for yourself. Mend yourself. Be yourself.

You are what the world needs. Not another baker's dozen of drama drones flying in with the latest shade of lavender or mint. Combed fully through, bright thick smile, waiting for the next upgrade.

Do you see that? There's a road there, unpaved. Yes, that one. I know, it looks like work, it looks overgrown and grueling but baby, it's worth it. It leads to so much more. Don't ask me, just lace those shoes tight and forget the phone.

I promise you, you can't tag your location anyway.

BLUFF

I'm highly contagious.
I'm a tortured soul.
I've got your spilt personality.
I'm your hard-earned cash.
The Mary Jane stash.
I'm your blockade.
The snow storm in the middle of June.
The queen of hearts up my sleeve.
I break them.
Hearts I mean.

Summer always reminds me of
every mistake I made
and spring of
everybody's bed I've laid.
As we lie in covers as two new lovers,
and lie to each other
hoping that no one came before
and no one will come after.
Though we know each of us
has lived decades of lives before
and will probably love
and live decades more without.

The possibilities are endless,
when you pretend to have no doubt.

THE EVOLUTION OF DATING

I'm the one you now tell your girlfriends about.
The one who scarred the inner deep in you.
The one who doesn't allow you to love like they do.

I'm the one you rip apart to your family now.
The one who is the joke at the dinner table.
The one who you loved but now, are not able.

I'm the one you remind your friends about.
The one who *(remember)* she did that and this.
The one who *(you know)* didn't know how to kiss.

I'm the one who now has no introduction.
The one who is a thought you'd rather not have.
The one who was a sweet treat
but now the taste is all bad.

Because I corrupted your view.
Because I left you.
And now it's I,
who doesn't know what to say about you.

Who said you weren't beautiful
or smart
or necessary
or potent
or vast?

Who said you weren't capable
or fire
or heart
or bone
or breath?

"Who said."
"Who?"
"Yeah. Who."

But baby, not TRUTH.

ERROR PRAYER

I'm the whore du jour.
I'm the virgin birth
of discrete longing.
I'm sorry for the tears
and I'm broken for your lost years.

I'm the heartbreaker
of a thousand men
and they don't even know it yet.

I don't revel in it.
It doesn't become me.
I know it.
I own it.

QUEEN KONG

She doesn't mind stairs
but she'd rather walk floors.
Perhaps layer each level
like a sandwich and savoy it slow.
Only to find
she's consumed an entire building.
The block, now unrecognizable,
with an indescribable
blank of space.
She stops,
she smiles
and raves about its taste.

TRAVEL

Anywhere
and
everywhere
you go
people will still be
walking their dogs
and
ordering bad coffee.

FOUR THE MEN

Men work,
yet thirst deeply for something else.
And they can't trigger it.
They can't find the button
and can't deny its power.
Making them powerless.
They don't like this
and they look for it in me.
In them, I could be.
I wish I would be for them.
Both parties disappointed,
them brokenhearted.
Me, surprised my heart started.

I'd like to line them up in a room
and take memories from each one,
embrace their hatred of me
with sweet and apologetic shame.
Take the blame, say their name.
One last time.
Kiss their cheeks,
wipe the tears they couldn't hold back.
Tell them, it's okay.
And mean it.
Mean it, like knowing the blood from my heart
still provides for my useless body.
The one they loved at one point,
yet no longer.

I'm sorry.
I'm sorry.

I can't say it enough and *I mean it.*

I DON'T THINK ABOUT YOU MUCH ANYMORE

It's strange to be thrusted into another's life so quickly, then to become strangers even faster. I don't think about you much anymore.

Sometimes you are cologne that I pass by on the street or a side curved smile across the cheek. And years have gone by, some months too. No, I don't think about you much anymore.

I've started to forget how you breathed at night. The length of your fingers, the creases above your forehead. The gold fleck in your right eye that would catch the sun just right. No, I don't think about you much anymore.

The way you stuttered certain cities names with excitement and adventure. Like point A to point B was the journey you'd only want to take with me and you'd let me pick all the songs, while I dance around, singing lightly with the voice that soothed your wrongs. And you were wrong but then so was I.

Instead of letting each other wrap the wounds like two soldiers in the trenches. We decided to cut deeper. To listen less. To jaggedly operate on each other's already mutilated souls like two people with something to prove. Prove that we were meant to be alone. Wildly creative and independent, like those artists you read about from the 19th century. The ones that went crazy from toxic paint. Went insane from being suffocated by what they'd create.

I think about how I regret not touching your hair more, not grabbing your hand close, not feeling your heartbeat inside the locked cage of rib you hid behind. I never listened to you, because I was too busy trying to be something you could fall in love with but it was never me. I was never me. I was just the stars I'd see when I rubbed my eyes to get rid of reality. But you were real to me and quickly as we separated, we did collide.

I think about you all the time now.
I'm sorry, I lied.

MORNING SOUND

Did you know that laughs can be an ache?
Hearing the deep and colliding waves
of true rich happiness,
can cause a quake of sublime textures
of willing and unwillingness.
The kind that you don't want to fall under.
Like a curtain of velvet, smooth and yet heavy.
Cascading slowly down
to the tips of every part of your body.
The parts that you didn't know were alive.
The parts so far down to the root of bitterness.
Locked up tight under a vault of fear.
A laugh can be an ache.
A throbbing awareness of a possible removal from it.

His is a foggy stream of memory.
One that has sat there for so long, unaware.
Now it has structure and space.
It's arrived at the station.
His laugh is now a developed sensation
that I can't ever lose.
I can't.

He says I shouldn't need things.
But this, this I need.

I can write like this.
I can sew together words like fluid garlands.
Reaching him across the miles and he'll find out.
That he too needs.

Come my love.
I'll lead.

BROKE IN PEACE, HIS

They don't have time to catch up to me.
These words that bruise the bottom of his jaw.
Like a fist of fallen doves, these fighting gloves.
Their pulses high and deep,
a rushing river of unapologetic heat.
Spew, spit, repeat.
I am a linguist of liability.
Unreliability.
Deniability.

Who would want to learn this language?
Who would want to sit through this lecture?
Its texture is starchy and coarse,
full of stingy remorse.
The words are the sticks and stones.
The tones of a dire frequency,
this delinquency is frightening.

Who wants to be alone long enough with me
to get a battle scar?
The ones you can brag to your friends about.
How this little girl's shouts blow the house down.
I don't own a crown, but my words are king.
I'm not one for guns, but I do all the firing.

They don't call me
by my given name anymore.
I don't ask them to,
they don't know a difference
but I do.
The men chanted it.
Like rope
wrapping me around
with their weight
and carnage.
Pushed out by tongue.
Pulled in by temper.

I suffocated nightly
to the heated lies
of its letters connected
like the cord
my mother and I shared.
That moment when she birthed me
and I became.
When she first spoke my name.
It, soaking with promise.
One that I couldn't keep.
I let too many men play with it.
Wrap it around their tongue.
Spew it out like gasoline
on the fire,
until done.

I'VE GOT A RIDDLE

Life does not describe this nor tailor it correctly.
There are no words in language
that can knit together verses
that would pronounce it into understanding.
It is resounding.
Weightless and ripe.

A memory you remember but never had.
It is not created by time,
as time cannot contain it, delay it.
It is the persistence,
the fourth meal,
the long-lost movie reel.
It is the breath between,
the air around that is present but forgotten.
It has fought in war,
won hands down and asked for more.

The tourniquet,
the vulnerable nighttime
that holds you above the earth's calamity.
It is the battery,
the ripened bosom of safety.
It elates me.
Doesn't mistake me, for I'm begotten.
It is sought in the deepest depths
of the human soul.
There is a gentle pull that ignites soft fires.
It may tire but only because it's been running
through your mind all day.

The only description that could touch
even a small part of its surface
is its purpose to warm
the hands of your heart like a glove,
today it is the prescription,
a homeopathic drug.

It is love. *This is love.*

NEW LOVE

It's only an eye.
The ball of it,
the pupil pressed clearly to one side.
The posture of the lash,
up and open.

Frozen on me like a thousand spotlights.
The crease of incredible.
The brow tangible to my dreams.
The one with mended seams.
Sewn together by many ties.

Don't you wink.
Don't you remain fixed on me.
I'll fall like a tree and you will gather my leaves.
Yet, you will still see me living,
attached to the branches of my battered lungs.
Please look at me like you do.
Look at me forever and then some.

THERAPY

Our time is up.
One hour on the dot.
Connect the dots.
It's a puppy dog.
The kind you wanted
when you were a kid.
The kind you got.
The kind that got ran over
the day you turned six
and realized how you lose things.

And I'm not talking about your keys.

SECOND HELPINGS

You firsts of the world.
The ones strutting naively down the streets.
These bars that produce you
spilling out of your sequined tops
and thin black tights.

Coming from a graduated second,
I look compelled but in complete amazement
how you don't break down in tears most of the time.
All that attention.
The drool the boys leave, that you step in
in your four-inch heeled boots
on your way to the grungy, graffiti-ed bathroom.
But it's their hunger you're after.

To be the pack of wolves' next slab of meat
complete with an already slurred speech
and heavy weighted feet that fling wildly
and rhythmically to the jungle beat
that collapses people left and right into tangled
messes on the dance floor.
I have realized that none of these men,
that grunt and gallop wildly like animals,
see me.

Nonetheless, I will still join in the stampede.
Get tossed like a wave on this human sea
and hope that someone, somewhere
will throw a net out one day to catch me.
For I may not be a three.
Nor a one.
But to someone
(it'll be enough.)

AIR

My heart was longing for you suddenly
and I became short of breath.
The kind you took away so long ago
and only gave back what little I have left.

HI AGAIN

It doesn't go away, it finds me.
When I turn the corners on sidewalks.
That third bite of lunch.
The vibration of my toothbrush.
The left sock, the last button.
Deep in the pockets
and under the layers,
it finds me.

And I don't run.
Maybe this will be fun this time.
I can make friends with my former self.
See her numb.
She didn't have problems.
She enjoyed the freedom of survival
and the luxury of whiplash.

When does talking about this become boring?
What if I never talk about it?
What if it just drips down
to puddles around my shoes?
I can get used to being wet all the time.
Colds form this way.
I can be sick for pleasure.
Sick to get time off.
Then maybe I can finally hide from it.

Because it keeps finding me.
In the routine of the hours.
It finds me being busy,
when I don't have any more power.

SOCIAL

I wonder how tiring
striving
for perfection is.

Posting the good angles
only.
Making the mundane
holy.

Putting pedestals
under coffee mugs
and lunch dishes.

Like we haven't seen food.
Yet,
in this light.
But,
with these people.

How exhausting to perform
daily.
Living life in celebrity,
with no resume.

Starving for
reactions.
With pleasing
distractions.

They are our oxygen.
Yet I ask,
but what then?

The legacy scrolled up.
The reality rolled down.

What are you leaving
but dirty
coffee
grounds?

And then I realize
how I too
thirst for it.
I drink from it.
I too sink in.

Let it eat
away
the
bone.

I wonder how tiring
striving
for perfection is.

Then I remember...

I haven't
slept
in years.

BREAKFAST

You say I'm reaching
for branches that can't be touched.
I think I'm just waiting
for your flesh to shut up.
Your sermon is not
making new friends with myself.
It's pushing and cheating
at a hand it hasn't been dealt.
I'm giving out cards,
but your hand shows you've too many.
Your face realizes the work you've loaded
and you're not ready.
I've put all my chips in.
But the fact is, I'm losing.
I'm dripping with all this love
and you're on the couch snoozing.

REGRETS TO INFORM

I don't want another love lost,
Bing Bang, tortured soul,
Kill that feeling in my heart,
Suffocate, wanna date?
Only after we say hello.

SOOTHE YOUR TEMPER TANTRUM

I encourage you to put down the consumer driven visuals and air waves of mass media clogging the arteries of your heart, preventing it from feeling and understanding true beauty and creation. That you do not hunger merely for affirmations of others and yet feast on it gluttonously from your own thoughts and ideas.

I wish the things you own and the purchases you have made to not showcase the true value you have on yourself. That you find real riches in the oddities and observations of human life, in the dignity of struggle and then the wisdom that births intensely from it.

I need you to know your worth. That the person you've always wanted to be is in fact already you and ever changing and the person you want to be with is attainable and in reach. That you deserve both and with great elation and claim, like the land you've been inhabiting your whole life, is yours for the taking.

I desire you to feel eagerly and vastly the openness of the city, the turbulent height of every building and the immense length of every street. The opulent and historic architecture that was once a vision, then a drawing, then a sweat filled lifetime of many dreamers all crafting passion with patchwork and desire with depth and form.

I crave you to know love. The kind that buries its head in your chest, pounds heartbeats down to your toes, drumming out words read by heated whispers and sleepy sonnets. The ember of a soothing stare that calms the storms, yet the flame of a feverish stir that quakes the body into submission and then solitude.

I hope you see that the sun rises just for you and the moon shyly winks you to sleep every night. That the stars cluster and burst light at the sound of your speech. The rhythm of your veins and the curves of your face gravitates the supernovas to form in your honor.

I pray you believe every word you read here. That the sentences written with urgency and anticipation grow gardens in your mind that you will water, because you believe in their importance. And you believe the beauty they produce is created and succeeds inside you first. That you pick those flowers grown and share them with people. Even if they don't deserve it, even if they have shown you only hate. Bloom bouquets for humanity.

Leave no one behind.
Be wise, be lovely, be giving, be kind.

Made in the USA
Columbia, SC
08 May 2020